When Your Grandparent Dies

A Child's Guide to Good Grief

Written by
Victoria Ryan

Illustrated by
R. W. Alley

ONE
CARING
PLACE

Abbey Press
St. Meinrad, IN 47577

In memory of
R. Eileen Ganz.
I love you, Mom.

Text © 2002 Victoria Ryan
Illustrations © 2002 St. Meinrad Archabbey
Published by One Caring Place
Abbey Press
St. Meinrad, Indiana 47577

Library of Congress Catalog Number
2002100909

ISBN 978-0-87029-364-1

Printed in the United States of America

A Message to Parents, Teachers, and Other Caring Adults

As an adult, you understand the enormous heartbreak caused by the death of a loved one. You have the maturity, reasoning, language development, and network of friends to help you cope. None of these coping strategies is available to a grieving child, though. It's up to caring adults to support children through the grieving process.

First and foremost, we need to acknowledge that the child's grief is real. Involve your child in the funeral. Taking flowers to the altar or drawing a picture of Grandma to put in the casket can help your child to feel connected. If the funeral and burial have already taken place, the child can still take flowers to the cemetery or add his name to the thank-you notes.

Recognize that grief looks different at different ages. A very young child will not understand the permanency of death and will expect Grandpa to be alive again in a day or two. Her sadness may not be apparent until weeks later when she is tired of waiting to see Grandpa. An older child will understand the permanency of death all too well, even to the point of logically concluding that "if Grandma died, then Mom or Dad or I could die too."

Be prepared for exaggerated behavior. A usually quiet child may become all the more withdrawn; an active child may seem out of control. Think of non-punishing ways to deal with the behavior—for example, arrange more outside time for the active child, more one-on-one time with the quiet child. Try to keep your child's routine as close to normal as possible to reassure her that everything is under control.

Give grieving children permission to talk, cry, laugh, and play. Let them see that people can comfort each other. Encourage them to keep their grandparent's spirit alive through a special keepsake or memorial scrapbook. In doing so, you will show your child not only how to mourn, but how to begin again.

May the spirit of your child's grandparent be especially close to each of you—to comfort you and guide you through grief.

—Victoria Ryan

Everybody Is Sad

When your grandparent is very sick, your whole life can seem mixed up. Your mom may cry a lot, and your dad may be very quiet. Your brother or sister may look worried. Your aunt and uncle call every day. Nobody smiles much. Nobody laughs.

Your mom or dad may say, "Your grandparent's time is near." That means your grandparent is going to die very soon.

It is a sad, sad time.

Saying Good-bye

If your mom and dad take you to see your grandparent, you hope he or she will be the same as always. But your grandparent might look different and may not be able to talk.

There might be tubes to carry medicine into your grandparent's body and special machines around the bed.

It's good to hug your grandparent and say, "I love you." Your grandparent will feel your hug and hear your special words.

It's Okay to Cry

When a grandparent dies, you miss him or her very much. Your grandparent gave you a special kind of love. He or she always had time for you, listened to you, and was proud of you. Your grandparent laughed and had fun with you.

You might feel tears in your eyes, but you don't want to be a baby. It's okay to cry. It doesn't matter if you're a boy or a girl or how old you are. It's okay not to cry too.

Not everybody acts sad in the same way. Your little cousins might run around the house and make a lot of noise. Your younger sister may cry one minute, then play a game the next. Your older brother may just tell you to leave him alone.

What Dying Means

When your parents say that your grandparent "died," it means your grandparent's body stopped working and cannot be fixed.

Death happens to all living things—flowers and frogs, goldfish and gerbils, dogs and cats, and people.

But a person is more than just a body. A person also has a "spirit." This is the part of you that laughs and loves and makes friends with people. It's what makes you YOU.

Though your grandparent's body has died, his or her spirit is still alive, in heaven with God.

Heaven

Heaven is a beautiful place where God takes care of people when they die. There is no pain or sickness in heaven. Your grandparent will always be happy there.

Talk with your mom and dad about what heaven might be like. Do you think your grandmother might be baking cookies there? Do you think your grandfather could be fishing?

People in heaven cannot visit earth, and you cannot visit heaven. But you can feel your grandparent's spirit whenever you think of his or her special love for you. Your love for each other goes on forever.

Crazy Feelings

You might have strange, new feelings you've never had before. These new feelings may surprise you and confuse you.

You might wonder why other kids are so happy when you are so sad. You might feel so angry that you want to go outside and break big sticks in the backyard. You might want to run and run until the strange feelings go away.

When your friends call, you don't feel like talking. Even if your dog tugs on your pants leg, you don't want to play catch. Your aunt might offer to buy you a super-duper banana split, but you aren't hungry. You are tired, but can't fall asleep. You wonder if you'll ever feel good again.

It's Not Your Fault

Maybe you think it's your fault that your grandfather died, because you acted up while he was sick. Maybe you feel guilty because you stayed at your friend's house instead of visiting your grandmother.

There might even have been things about your grandparent you did not like. Maybe your grandparent talked too loudly, or smelled funny, or told you to stand up straight all the time.

Your grandparent's death is *not* your fault. You did *not* make your grandparent die—and you can *not* make your grandparent "un-die," even if you act very, very good.

The Scariest Feeling of All

When a grandparent dies, it can also make you feel afraid.

You might be afraid to go into your grandparent's house again. Or you may suddenly be scared that your dog will get lost. Mostly you are afraid that your mom or dad will die, as your grandparent did. You might even be worried that you will die.

Most people live a long, long time. And there will always be someone to love and take care of you.

Talking Helps

Talking about your feelings with your parents or another grown-up can help you to feel better. If you don't know what to say, they will help you find the words.

You might want to make up a story, song, or poem about your feelings. You could draw a picture of special times you spent with your grandparent—like picking out pumpkins, watching fireworks, or making pancakes.

You can make a Memory Book or a Keepsake Box—for pictures, cards, and other things that remind you of your grandparent.

What Is a Funeral?

Family and friends get together at a "funeral" to honor someone who has died.

Many funerals start at a special place called a "funeral home." Lots of people come to visit your family there. They say nice things about your grandparent. They tell you they are sorry your family is sad.

They may also look at your grandparent's body. It will be in a special box called a "casket," and it will be very still and cold. But you will know that your grandparent's spirit is alive and happy in heaven.

The Funeral Service

Your family may have a special funeral "service." People will pray, sing, and read from holy books. Some might give speeches about your grandparent.

Then your family will take the casket with the body to the "cemetery." A cemetery is a peaceful place where people's bodies are buried. The casket is put on a special part of the lawn called the "grave." A beautiful rock with your grandparent's name on it will be put on the grave later—to remind everyone how much your family loved your grandparent.

Afterward, you will probably go back to your house, where there will be lots of food and talking. Your family may tell funny stories about your grandparent. Remembering your grandparent and laughing will help you to feel better.

Listen and Learn

When people talk about the funny, kind, or brave things your grandparent did in life, listen closely.

You may learn about how things were when your grandparent was a child. You may find out that your grandparent got into trouble—just like you do sometimes. You will hear about why people loved your grandparent so much.

Ask people how they knew your grandparent. Find out what they liked best about him or her. Ask if you are like your grandparent in any way.

How Long Will You Be Sad?

Soon after the funeral, you will go back to school. Your parents will go back to work. But you can't always go right back to feeling happy.

You may try to read a book, but your mind will be thinking about other things. When the phone rings, you might think it's your grandparent—until you remember that your grandparent is in heaven.

These sad feelings are called "grief." Grief will go away a little each day, but you have to help make it leave. How? Think about what your grandparent would want you to do...

What Your Grandparent Wants

Your grandparent worked hard, helped people, loved family, and had fun with friends. Your grandparent had to face some big problems in life—like not having enough money, losing a job, or fighting a war. And, like you, your grandparent probably had to deal with the death of a grandparent.

Even so, your grandparent enjoyed life and lived it well—and wants you to do the same.

Love your family. Work hard. Be a good friend. Help people. Have fun. You will feel happy then. And that is just what your grandparent would want.

Victoria Ryan holds a master's degree and national certification in speech-language pathology. She works primarily with school-age children, and teaches reading and composition at the college level. A writer and workshop speaker on writing-related topics, she has published works in the areas of communication, grief, and family. She and her husband have six sons and live in Hamilton, Ohio.

R. W. Alley is the illustrator for the popular Abbey Press adult series of Elf-help books, as well as an illustrator and writer of children's books. He lives in Barrington, Rhode Island, with his wife, daughter, and son. See a wide variety of his works at: www.rwalley.com.